SEARCHING FOR THE

Holy Grill

The Most Divine Burgers in Minnesota, Wisconsin & Iowa

**Written and Illustrated by
Jeff Hagen**

Adventure Publications, Inc.
Cambridge, Minnesota

For Kit and Mary and Cynthia

Cover and interior design by Jonathan Norberg

Copyright 2003 by Jeff Hagen

ISBN: 1-59193-008-1

Published by Adventure Publications, Inc.
820 Cleveland St. S
Cambridge, MN 55008
800.678.7006

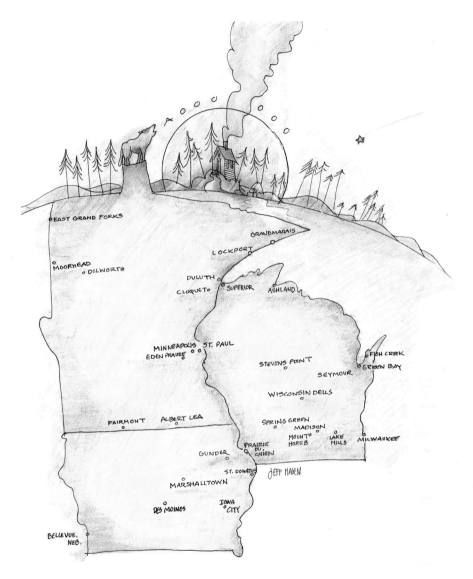

EAST GRAND FORKS

GRANDMARAIS

LOCKPORT

MOORHEAD   DILWORTH

DULUTH

CLOQUET   SUPERIOR   ASHLAND

MINNEAPOLIS ST. PAUL
EDEN PRAIRIE

STEVENS POINT

FISH CREEK

SEYMOUR   GREEN BAY

WISCONSIN DELLS

FAIRMONT   ALBERT LEA

SPRING GREEN
MADISON

MOUNT
HOREB   LAKE
MILLS   MILWAUKEE

GUNDER

PRAIRIE
DU
CHIEN

ST. DONATUS   JEFF HAGEN

MARSHALLTOWN

DES MOINES   IOWA
CITY

BELLEVUE,
NEB.

WHERE'S THE BEEF?!

TABLE OF CONTENTS

The Sampler
Holy Cow! Burger Trivia

- The average American (of all ages) eats three hamburgers a week.

- One third of all Americans have eaten a burger within the past 24 hours.

- 86 percent of the population ordered a hamburger or cheeseburger in 2002.

- 59 percent of all sandwiches sold in America are hamburgers.

- Hamburgers comprise 71 percent of beef servings in commercial restaurants in 2001.

- 8.2 billion burgers were served in restaurants in 2001.

- Burgers account for 40 percent of all sandwiches sold.

- 65 percent of all burgers served in 2001 were consumed away from home.

- The Hamburger Hall of Fame is in Seymour, Wisconsin. (Read all about it on page 86!)

- McDonald's has served 12 hamburgers for every person in the world.

- The first hamburger chain, which opened its first stand in 1921 in Kansas, was White Castle. (Read all about it on page 88!)

- Hamburger doesn't contain ham. So where does the name come from? The word's roots trace back to Hamburg, Germany, where people ate a similar food, the Hamburg steak. When it arrived in the U.S., the slightly modified term "hamburger" was adopted.

- The Kiwis brought the world-renowned reputation of the Dairyland to the other side of the globe. If you're in the New Zealand area, sample the eats from Burger Wisconsin, a chain of '50s-style burger joints found all over the country. (Read all about it on page 90!)

O little town of Lipitor...

"Jeff, this book could kill you," my doctor and old friend warned me. "After doing those fish fry books, your cholesterol level is higher than that of a medium-sized American city."

So, it was with that forewarning and my daily regime of Lipitor and exercise that I embarked upon the mission of this book: the quest for the best grill in the upper Midwest.

The method to discovery

My method of operation was simple: I drove to various points on my Minnesota, Wisconsin and Iowa state maps. I randomly chose a center of humanity, traveled to it, stopped and asked various people in grocery stores, gas stations, and town squares this basic question: Where is the best place to get a hamburger around here?

I didn't ask newspaper food critics or gourmet "experts" for their five-star recommendations for this book. I went further into the heart and soul of America—I asked the common man on the street. I asked the true pathfinders—truck drivers and savvy travelers who frequent the back-roads and byways of the upper Midwest, as well as the locals and waitresses who dined with and served them. If the same name came up more than twice, I would head out to the place and dine with the locals in the confort of their favorite Holy Grill.

I heard the tales of their favorite spot and its legendary hamburger like no other in the land. On my journey, I found that Burgerland, U.S.A. is a much larger culinary continent than I had ever dreamed. As one vast grill that stretches across the land, its sizzle can be heard in Green Bay, Albert Lea and Grand Marais. The aroma of fried onions and melted cheese wafts above the city streets in Minneapolis, Milwaukee and Iowa City.

My journey took me to over 150 places to chow down on legendary local burgers. Of these, 37 are truly worth driving to. Though different in locations and sizes ranging from small-town drive-ins, city taverns and urban diners, they all share one common denominator; they all serve their own interpretation of the "best burger on Earth."

The jewels of the journey

I found the legendary "Jucy Lucy" hamburger of south Minneapolis. I found the largest hamburger ever cooked, weighing four tons and setting a Guinness World Record at the Hamburger Hall of Fame in Seymour, Wisconsin. I found a bar in a small town of 28 people that has a legendary burger so big (a pound and a half) and so popular that the bar goes through 100 pounds of fresh ground beef a day!

I found that every grill has its own legendary nickname for their claim-to-fame unique burger. On one jaunt, I sampled the Zip Burger, the Gunderburger, the Viking Burger, the S.O.B. (South of the Border) Burger and the Waz Burger. I also came across a place that serves a $29 hamburger. That burger is NOT in this book. In fact, its place in the history of the TRULY American Hamburger is a dubious footnote, at best.

This book is...

The REAL HAMBURGER is a common fare for common folk, as iconic to our culture as faded blue jeans and apple pie. That is what this book is all about. I searched for those places in the Heartland that have no pedigree, pretense or pomposity. This is a book for the common man in pursuit of that American icon eaten at least three times a week: the American Hamburger and its tasty derivatives.

The Lockport Marketplace & Deli
Land of the lumberjack

Casey Jones was here

Minnesota's North Shore is a wild and rugged stretch of scenery that is just teeming with historic legend and lore. Tucked away along the North Shore is the tiny one-building settlement of Lockport.

A century ago, the town thrived in the prosperity of the lumber industry. Lockport originated as a port for lumber boats to dock and load freshly cut virgin white pines from the Sawtooth Mountains that loom above the lake. Back then the pines were in bountiful abundance and the riches seemed endless.

That prosperity prompted a local entrepreneur to embark upon a risky and bold venture. He built a railroad that stretched from waters' edge far up into the mountains to haul the wood out at a profitable pace.

The railroad line was carved out of the woods and rock, the tracks were laid, and a huge steam engine was transported up north by boat to begin operation, that wasn't an easy task to complete in this deep Boreal Timber Country. But muscle and will power overcame the obstacles of nature and the Moose Mountain Railroad Line was completed.

A great celebration and festival kicked off the railroad. Speeches and toasts were made. The proud engine puffed up the mountain and came back down with a load of logs. The first day of operation was a roaring success! In jubilation, the owner of the railroad shipped off to Duluth to celebrate. It was, after all, his day to shine.

But, fate had another plan. Before the sun rose that man was murdered and neither he nor his railroad saw the next dawn. The railroad closed after ONE DAY of operation.

For years, the old engine sat on the dock, slowly rusting and falling apart until it finally was cut up for scrap. The town gradually shrank in size and all but faded from life. That was until 1928, when one Charley (Casey) Jones, a professional baseball player for the White Sox, built this roadside inn to coincide with the opening of the new highway that wound past Lockport on its way to the Canadian border.

Today it is owned by Nan Plude-Bradley and Deb Niemisto—two creative and friendly women who dish up North Shore hospitality, humor, and a hamburger that's well on its way to becoming a legend, way up here in a land where the tales are as tall as the timber.

EATS
A deli variety

Now remember, this is a deli. The grill is used for burgers, as well as thick Fur Trading French Toast and grilled focaccia sandwiches brushed with garlic butter. Deb's Finnish grandmother handed down her recipe for Finnish pastries, more than worth a try.

BEEF TIPS

Get the Deluxe Burger: a half-pound burger topped with bacon, cheddar, and their special sauce. For dessert, my suggestion is the Mocha Moose Brownie which has enough calories to carry you all the way to the Twin Cities. Take a seat in the outdoor eating area for a nice view à la carte.

5362 West Hwy 61 (On the lake side of Hwy 61 south of Grand Marais)
Lutsen, MN • 218.663.7548 • Open daily 7 a.m.–10 p.m.

My Sister's Place
Up north, just south of the border

THE SCOOP   Dine in the company of family

My Sister's Place is owned and operated by Anna Hamilton who, not coincidentally, has a sister who owns and operates the Trail Center, another great bar and grill up on the Gunflint Trail.

The atmosphere at My Sister's Place is northern rustic and very cozy. A row of buffalo plaid shirts and jackets permanently reside on the pegs of the coat rack. The walls are lined with antiques, hides, washtubs and photographs of...what else? Sisters.

It's a tradition to take a photograph of sisters who pick this place to wine and dine. Each new photograph is added to the collection of sister pictures that adorns the bar's interior. This is an extremely comfortable place to sit down and enjoy good company and good eats.

If you're seeking variety from the conventional burger, here's a very unique place for you to experience on your next trip north.

EATS   Variety is the spice of life

My Sister's Place in Grand Marais, Minnesota, offers hungry customers 28 types of hamburgers! Those in that vast stockyard of beef selection include:

The Jack Daniels Burger, the Philly Burger, Clifford's Goober Burger, Betty's Chicken Fried Burger, the Bull Moose Burger, the Hawaiian Burger, the Blue Boy Burger, the North Shore Burger, and a North Woods version of the "Jucy Lucy."

If you're doing the math, you'll realize that there is much more left on the burger list than this sampling. It's quite obvious that this place requires several visits (and a 55-gallon drum of Lipitor).

The only stress comes from decision making:

"Now, WHICH BURGER am I going to try tonight?"

Got a non-conformist in your group who doesn't want a burger this time? This place has 14 different kinds of hot dogs (call it Dog World!) and a separate list of speciality sandwiches. Knock yourself out! But keep in mind that this is the last good burger place before crossing the U.S.-Canadian border.

410 East Hwy 61 (P.O. Box 248), 30 miles south of the Canadian border
Grand Marais, MN • 218.387.1915
Open Sun–Thurs 11 a.m.–9 p.m. • Fri & Sat 11 a.m.–10 p.m.

Gordy's Hi-Hat

Hat trick

Go north!

So, what really makes a good hamburger? I mean a REALLY GOOD HAMBURGER!? To find the answer, I traveled far into the North Country to a place that I had heard about for years.

Gordy's Hi-Hat in Cloquet, Minnesota, is home of the best burger in the North.

I heard about Gordy's and its famous burger from people miles away in Minneapolis and Madison. The word on the city streets and 'burbs of Minneapolis was that if you have a cabin up north, Gordy's is a must stop on the commute to the lake.

"Forty to fifty percent of our customers are out-of-towners in transit to their lake cabins," reports owner Dan Lundquist.

EATS For which they flock from miles around

"Well, what makes this burger so special?" I asked.

Dan gave me a lesson in burger edification. "We do everything by hand here. We prepare our hamburgers every morning using fresh ground beef. We use an ice cream scooper and pat the patties. Hamburgers that are prepared by hand taste better."

"Why?" I asked.

"It's a simple fact; hand-formed burgers have more texture and aeration, which allows the juices to flow through the meat, creating a tastier burger than machine-stamped burgers found in hamburger chains. It's labor intensive work to make a hand-patted burger, but the whole family chips in. On average we go through 400 pounds of beef a day. That's 2,000 burgers!

"This is a family operation. Everybody from my dad (Gordy) and mom (Marilyn) to the grandchildren work here. We're extremely busy from our opening in March until season close in October.

In particular, opening day is one of the busiest days of the year.

"Some days, we go through 650 pounds of beef."

People flock here in annual rites of spring migration, like geese flying home to a place where northern pines usher in soft spring breezes, and the sweet aroma of onion rings drifts above melting snow.

(BEEF TIPS)

Try the homemade onion rings with your burger. It's the call of the wild!

415 Sunnyside Drive • Cloquet, MN 55720 • 218.879.6125
Open mid-March–first week of Oct 10 a.m.–9 p.m. (or until the last customer leaves)

Ray's Grill & The North Pole Bar
A polar adventure

One of the unexpected discoveries that I encountered on my search for the Holy Grill was the realization that some of the best burger places in the Midwest can be found right down the block in your neighborhood.

Ray's Grill & North Pole Bar is one such spot. Located in a blue-collar neighborhood in west Duluth, Ray's Grill offers no pretention, no glamour, no culinary fame. This simple bar & grill has something better: a great reputation that stretches back through time and generations of west Duluth neighbors who have dined here for over 35 years.

Advertising? Ray's has nothing but the best: word of mouth. While I was in Duluth, I asked people on the street where I could find the Holy Grill, and Ray's Grill consistently came up as the place to go.

Once I arrived at Ray's, I sat down with a couple of natives and asked them, "Why does this place have such a great reputation?"

Lee and Rose Englund, two local school teachers, offered this answer: "We grew up in Duluth, and this has always been a reliable spot to eat. A come-as-you-are place that has much more character and tradition than the typical, sterile hamburger franchise drive-thru in the suburb. It's a kick-back, fun eatery that simply offers a relaxing atmosphere and a great hamburger. It works for us. "After trying the burger here, I'm inclined to agree. Ray's is a working class bar that works for me.

As I let my eyes wander about the menu, it became clear to me that one of Ray's many allures is to feed its regulars something different from visit to visit. Casual dining items range from Italian sausage on a bun and cold deli sandwiches to spaghetti and meatballs and a hot pork sandwich, just like mom used to make. But of course, some people may be tempted to order a burger from Ray's every day of the week.

And speaking of which, order a Big Boss Double Burger—two quarter pound patties on a bun complete with bacon, lettuce, tomato and cheese.

5610 Raleigh Street • Duluth, MN • 218.628.1865
Open Mon–Sat 8 a.m.–2 p.m.

Whitey's Café

A horseshoe-shaped impression

Acquiring favorite restaurants often originates from the first of many repeat visits. The first impression is critical. And to make a great lasting first impression, you have to be 5-out-of-4-star good.

That is Whitey's, glowing bright in this growing northern Red River Valley border town of East Grand Forks, Minnesota. This marvelous café will win its way into your heart, but not just through your stomach.

THE SCOOP   Blazing neon forever

When North Dakota went dry during the Prohibition in the '20s, Minnesota bar owners near the border could take advantage of certain unquenchable vices. Edwin "Whitey" Larson seized the opportunity at only age 19, opening the Coney Island Lunch Room. Specializing in boot-leg alcohol, slot machines and hot dogs, it was a dwarf in comparison to the 40 nightclubs and restaurants in East Grand Forks.

But Whitey's success allowed him to buy a building on DeMers Avenue and to build the country's first stainless steel horseshoe bar in 1930, designed by local architect Samuel DeRemer. Whitey's Wonderbar— decked out in plush booths and mirrors that reflect the warm glow of neon—was featured in the Saturday Evening Post and Time Magazine for its Art Deco style.

Over time, the image that attracted gamblers and drinkers evolved into one that appealed to law-abiding citizens of every kind: from lawyers and priests to farmers and construction workers. Whitey's new focus was on serving excellent food, and because of this maturation, Whitey's was able to stand the test of time. It is now the last blazing neon light on a block that once had the highest concentration of neon lights in a three-block radius of any place in the world.

But more changes were in store for this café. For this entire area. This city—among many others in the Red River Valley—was devastated by the Flood of '97. Whitey's, just blocks from the sandbagged Red River, was swamped with close to six feet of water on the main floor.

But this community's spirit of faith kept alive a dream that Whitey envisioned in 1925. The Wonderbar was rebuilt in the new Whitey's, now a few buildings farther away from the river. It's a resounding flood recovery story the locals love to hear and tell. Their landmark is here to stay.

EATS
The tradition of excellence

Way up here on the way to Canada, it gets COLD. Forty below windchill in January is common, which means a staple of meat and potatoes to warm the belly is an absolute necessity for survival. Salads just don't make for good insulation (though the menu includes options for the light eater). In its continuing tradition of serving excellent food, Whitey's prides itself in serving an ever-changing menu, but hamburgers, steaks and Canadian walleye have been the classic favorites for years.

BEEF TIPS

That which won its way into my heart was the Wonder Burger, capped by lettuce, tomato, onions and special sauce.

121 DeMers Avenue • East Grand Forks, MN • 218.773.1831
Open daily 11 a.m.–10 p.m. • bar menu 10 p.m.–midnight

Hi Ho Tavern

Have a flashback

Certainly my quest for the Holy Grill became a test in recognizing signs of greatness that are not the blatantly obvious. The voices of the Fargo-Moorhead area coaxed me east of this college metropolis to Dilworth, Minnesota. There's not much to the town, not much to the storefront. This was a test.

The signs of greatness

I spoke to co-owner Rick Cariveau, who set the story's beginning in 1947: For 13 years, Glen Tollefson opened the doors of the Hi Ho Tavern. He said, "It was a name that originated from a night of brainstorming with a box of Hi Ho Crackers on his kitchen table.

"Back then he served nothing but 3.2 beer and burgers. I'm not even sure if they served a cheeseburger." But Glen unquestionably dished up a good time. The college kids would dodge homework in droves and make the trip east to Dilworth for a great burger that was easy on their scrappy budgets. "Customers 70 years old come in and tell stories of how much fun they used to have," Rick said.

Rick's folks, Earl and Edith, bought the place in 1960 and operated the same way until 1977. Rick and his wife Cathy then took ownership, and in 1996 the Cariveaus' son, Big Rick (he's taller than his dad, a.k.a. Old Man Rick), opened the Hi Ho South in south Fargo which serves the very same menu.

That's three generations of Cariveaus serving three generations of customers. But when it comes to burgers, there is no generation gap. "People gone for 30 years come back and say they can't believe it's the same burger they tasted in the '70s," Rick said. "We have a lot of repeat business, so obviously we're doing something right."

Now that's a sign of greatness.

The trick is to make a memorable burger and serve it at the same unbeatable price. Rick said, "We're still cooking our burgers on our seasoned grill the same way. We use the highest quality fresh beef from the same butcher, specially ground for the Hi Ho." Besides having the patties formed at the butcher shop instead of at the restaurant, nothing has changed since 1947. Not even the price: you can still feed a family of four for under 20 bucks.

Never underestimate the power of consistency, quality and price.

BEEF TIPS

Get the Hi Ho's Super Combo: your burger or sandwich with all the fountain soda you can drink and all the fries you can eat, all for under three dollars. I know! It's unheard of!

10 Center Avenue East • Dilworth, MN • 218.287.2975
Open Sat–Thurs 11 a.m.–10 p.m. • Fri 11 a.m.–11 p.m.

Mickey's Diner

Nothing could be finer than to be in Mickey's Diner

THE SCOOP Streamlined nostalgia

What could be more American to our country's grilling culture than the all-night diner? Their evolution stemmed from the portable sidewalk carts and street eateries of the turn of the century, emerging as full-service streamlined restaurants of the 1920s and 1930s.

Like urban lighthouses, they became reliable nocturnal sentinels on the darkest and stormiest of nights, and recognizable places to duck into in the wee hours of pre-dawn for breakfast or a sandwich.

Sadly, many of them have disappeared into history. But fortunately, this classic 1937 diner in downtown St. Paul has fired up its grill every day, every night of the year for the past 60 years. During Minnesota's famous blizzards or scorching heat waves, you can always count on Mickey's.

Added to the National Register of Historic Places in 1983, there is only one other diner of its kind listed as such. It's an urban marvel for young and old alike. As I sat down at the bar, I got lost in my senses—the alluring scent of my burger sizzling on the old grill, the bedazzling glass and streamlined structures emblazed by ruby red neon and gaudy circus color schemes, and the transporting power of Patsy Cline and Elvis belting the classics from a corner booth full of chatty kids.

This is the kind of timeless moment that only Mickey's can create.

EATS If it ain't broke, don't fix it

Mickey's isn't quite a sign of the times. They've stuck to the original plan, using pre-war recipes for their mulligan stew, baked beans and buttermilk pancakes. They still get their hamburger from the local butcher, bread from a St. Paul bakery and eggs from local farms. Hence, there is virtually no use for chemicals or preservatives in the food.

It doesn't get much better than this.

The burger to try at Mickey's is "The Big Erick." On a steamy summer day in the city, nothing will satisfy better than a tall glass of raspberry- or cherry-flavored phosphates topped with a dollop of whipped cream.

36 West Seventh Street • (Downtown) St. Paul, MN • 651.222.5633
Open 24 hours a day • 7 days a week

Andy's Garage

Honk twice for fries

The further I delved into learning about the origins and development of the American hamburger, the more I began to see that much of burger evolution centers around the wheel.

At the turn of the century the most popular hamburger vendor was the pushcart. That enterprise morphed into a larger hamburger stand, which was often an old trolley car converted into a sidewalk eatery. In the late 1920s and 1930s, The American diner came onto the scene. The most popular version was a chrome and glass streamlined version made in Wichita, Kansas (by Valentine Diners Inc.), and trucked across the U.S. to sit prominently alongside major highways, like the famous Route 66.

During the post-World War II era, the drive-in became very popular in America. In most towns and cities, the drive-in became the center of activity for the young, but also for the family with a station wagon filled with kids. Across America thousands of Mel's drive-in-style establishments throbbed with adolescent energy and dreams on any given weekend night.

Like a watering hole to wild mustangs, the drive-in attracted another emerging American icon: the hot rod.

THE SCOOP   Hot rods, hot burgers

Hot rods and burgers became synonymous with coast-to-coast American culture. So, I was tickled on my journey to come upon a cleverly converted temple of this culture: A hamburger emporium housed in a beautifully restored automobile service station and garage.

Andy's Garage is an eatery that was developed by Dee and Sande Traudt who saved the 1948 Skelly gas station from being demolished. After extensive renovation they renamed the old station after their daughter, Andy, and scheduled the restaurant's opening on her birthday.

The Traudt family has a flair for good food and a sensitivity for service to the community. Part of the station is a room devoted to community-centered activities, in effect keeping the heartbeat of the neighborhood alive. In the summertime Andy's opens its huge garage doors offering outdoor seating under a tent, and allowing the fresh summer breeze to cool its patrons inside.

At Andy's, you get good food and community involvement all wrapped up and served on a platter. Now that's truly an American service station.

EATS

Bring the kids!

Talk about kid-friendly: the juniors will go wild when you read "Kraft Mac & Cheese and PB&J" off their "Little Mechanics" menu. They'll stay occupied by looking for Mr. Potato Head, who is hidden somewhere in the diner. The tyke that finds him wins a special prize!

BEEF TIPS

Live music plays from 8–10 p.m. every Saturday night, so wear your blue suede shoes. Try the Andy Burger (The inside joke: the menu says it's her favorite, but Andy, who happened to be my waitress, said it's too big for her.) Test the corn fries, made of corn meal and served with salsa. It's a sweet marriage of the tortilla chip and the french fry, but resembling the latter. Then cool your tongue with a frosted mug root beer float.

1825 University Avenue (at University and Fairview Avenues) • St. Paul, MN
651.917.2332 • Open Mon–Thurs 7 a.m.–8 p.m. • Fri & Sat 7 a.m.–10 p.m.

Snuffy's Malt Shop

A classic American

THE SCOOP

Deeply rooted in American culinary culture is the Malt Shop. Sadly, many of the great malt shops of the past have disappeared. Much of their demise has to do with profit margins, changing trends and corporate control of confectionary outlets across the country.

Fortunately, for true diehards of the American Malt and Shake Shop, there are a few proud survivors out there in Ice Cream Land. Snuffy's in the Twin Cities is a small chain of malt and burger shops that honors the old tradition.

Walking in, I noticed a wall of framed Best Burger and Ice Cream Awards (one even from the stately New York Times). It's apparent from the acclaim and plaudits of the features displayed that this place is well respected in the eyes of food and travel writers. But, I witnessed a bigger tribute to Snuffy's than the New York Times: families...happy families.

On the day I visited Snuffy's, the place was filled with couples and their children. It was obvious, as I chomped down on my Snuffy Burger, that the atmosphere at Snuffy's is family-friendly. To me that's value and intrinsic magic that goes far beyond framed words.

EATS

No corners cut

So what is the secret behind the showcase wall of acclaim and plaudits? In the 20 years that Snuffy's has been in operation, they can proudly say that not one corner has been cut. They use real vanilla hard ice cream in their malts, sundaes and floats, which makes their old-fashioned malt none other than their bread and butter.

My suggestion is to try the Snuffy Burger coupled with your favorite malt. Hey! I've never claimed that this would be a diet book.

244 South Cleveland Avenue • Highland Park, MN • 651.690.1846
Open Mon–Sat 11 a.m.–9 p.m. • Sun 12 p.m.–9 p.m.

The Nook

By hook or by nook

Consider this: every town and city in America has its own version of the Sports Bar. Common stock and trade to the Sports Bar, they all claim to be the biggest and the brightest luminary in that vast galaxy of All-American watering holes. Well folks, they're all pale in comparison to this small unassuming storefront deep in the heart of St. Paul. For this is the ultimate sports bar. In terms of Sports Bars, this is the Holy Grill.

Look at its history and then look at its heart. The bar dates back to 1938 when it was known as Mickey's Nook, which was gifted with three blessings that make a business successful: location, location, location. The bar was located right across the street from the Cretin-Durham High School baseball field. To be fair, straight over the left field fence.

Now, during hot summer nights over all those years, that little baseball park has produced some tremendous athletes. Minnesota Twin Paul Molitor, and Paul Mauer, who in 2001 was the number one draft in the U.S. right out of high school, both played ball across the street from the Nook. Throw in Chris Weinke, who won the Heisman Trophy in 2000, former NFL player Steve Walsh and MLB umpire Tim Tschida, and you get an idea of the home talent caliber that graced this neighborhood ball park.

With all that talent and athletic muscle it was inevitable that many of those super athletes jacked home runs out of the park. Can you imagine where they were headed? That's right! The Nook!

Countless home runs launched by the likes of Molitor and others landed on the roof, canopy, and through the windows of the Nook, making this not a bar for the spectator, but rather for the active participant in the ball game going on across the street. Of course, a lot of these ball players congregate at the Nook, both young and old. It is a living sports bar that abounds in friendly stories and laughter of days past, balls hit and victorious games toasted in communal celebration.

This bar may seem small in dimension. But look again, for the Nook has a major league heart like no other.

Have you had your Nookie today?

According to co-owners Ted Jasper and Mike Runyon, the secrets of their success are threefold: first, their grill has been in use since 1948, and it only has an on/off switch. Not only will you be impressed by a perfect burger with the beauty of that old grill patina, but also by the cooking skills it takes to get it just right. Secondly, they only use Velveeta™ cheese. And lastly, they divinely blend their secret seasoning, and keep it a sacred mystery to the rest of us.

BEEF TIPS

I'll pass on the recommendation of Mike, who hit the bullseye with this one: get the Juicy Nookie Burger, which won Best Burger in the Twin Cities in 2003.

And find a seat AWAY from the window during baseball season.

492 Hamline Avenue South (near Randolph & Hamline Avenues) • St. Paul, MN
651.698.4347 • Open Sun–Thurs 10 a.m.–10 p.m. • Fri & Sat 10 a.m.–11 p.m.

Matt's Bar

We love Lucy

They beefed up the middle...with cheese

At this small corner bar on the south side of Minneapolis, the story told at the bar reaches back a half century ago when a customer started a legend. The guy had frequented the bar for years, typically ordering a cheeseburger along with his Grain Belt™ beer. One night he told the bartender/cook, "Surprise me. Make my usual UNUSUAL tonight."

So the cook took up the challenge. Instead of making a conventional cheeseburger with the cheese riding on top of the meat, he took two patties and added a slice of Kraft™ American cheese in the middle of the two pieces of meat. Sort of like an Oreo™ cookie of the hamburger world.

Well, needless to say, the old timer was impressed. Someone in the bar tagged the new burger with the moniker "Jucy Lucy" and a legend was born. (Yes, it's spelled without an "i." The printers misprinted the menus 50 years ago, and it stuck.)

Nowadays, it's the most popular hamburger on the south side. Several other bars have their own versions of the Jucy Lucy, but here it reigns supreme.

On the day that I stopped here, one of Matt's patrons who works for an ad agency had created a small sign that appeared on the wall with the proclamation, "Home of the Jucy Lucy: the Hamburger Equivalent to the Twinkie™!"

EATS

Dos and don'ts (mostly don'ts)

There are a few things that makes Matt's Bar a unique eating experience. First, Matt's menu is so concise, you can count the items on your two hands. It's clear what the crowd pleaser is; the award-winning Jucy Lucy works as a stand-alone. So don't ask for a menu, because it's not much of a list. Don't wear your Sunday best to Matt's either. Just plan on wearing a little Jucy Lucy home with you.

And don't ask for ice or a plate, just as another sign reads, "No ice. No plates. We blew it on napkins."

BEEF TIPS

Be careful when you bite into one of these little delights. The inside is still piping hot. My advice: sip a beer first and take this one slow. Life is too short to hurry a good hamburger experience. THIS IS the burger to which other grills look for inspiration.

3500 Cedar Avenue South • Minneapolis, MN • 612.729.9936
Open Mon–Wed 11 a.m.–12 a.m. • Thurs–Sat 11 a.m.–1 a.m. • Sun 12 p.m.–12 a.m.

Lion's Tap
The feast of Eden

Succcess in simplicity

Just outside of Eden Prairie, Minnesota, lies an unassuming tavern that has received more than a lion's share of awards and commendations for its hamburgers.

While waiting for my burger, I glanced up at the knotty pine wall and noticed a long gallery of framed magazine articles proclaiming that this roadside tavern has won a multitude of awards for the BEST burger in the Minneapolis metro area. One framed letter indicated that the Lion's Tap was selected as one of the Top 500 Restaurants in the United States. Pretty heady stuff for this place.

What's their secret to all this success? It's a simple list: one, it's a family-owned operation. (The Notermann family celebrated their 25th anniversary of ownership in 2002.) Two, the Notermanns use a secret seasoning recipe in their freshly ground beef. Three, they have loyal staff members who have worked here for years. And four, a dedicated group of true-blue customers descend on this Minnesota River bluff tavern daily.

Simple and true, it's easy to see why this place is so lionized in the eyes of Twin Cities burger fans.

EATS

Fit for a king

The Lion's Tap is a roadside establishment that focuses on flavor over frills. It's a simple menu at the Lion's Tap. The menu offers a short list of choices: hamburgers, french fries, pop, beer and milk. That's it. But by the looks of this busy establishment, people come in hoards for a guaranteed tasty burger made with the freshest ingredients. The lettuce and tomato tasted like they had their own garden in the backyard.

When out of the cluttered murmur of conversation between families and friends, you can make out proclamations like, "Ooh, that tasted good," or "Wow that was a good burger," you know you're in the right place.

I had the California Burger with a little pink inside. It might very well be the envy of California. They have great burgers and a great atmosphere, but be careful when pulling off the highway into Lion's Tap. It's a risky intersection, so use caution and be patient.

16180 Flying Cloud Drive • Eden Prairie, MN • 952.934.5299
Open Mon–Thurs & Sun 11 a.m.–10 p.m. • Fri & Sat 11 a.m.–11 p.m.

The Convention Grille

Home sweet home

THE SCOOP

Take their word for it

Families and people of all ages get a kick out of this beloved 1930s diner that has been so untouched since muscle shirts and poodle skirts. It really is a great conversation piece for those who journeyed through eras of change, all the while their hang-out seemed to have stood still. Continuity is what makes this place feel like home to many people.

The high-backed booths, cozy atmosphere and good food keep calling people back for generations, with many visiting every time they return to the Twin Cities. I decided to let the people who eat at the establishment speak for themselves and the café they love so much:

"My parents took me here as a kid. It was a big treat for me back then. Now as an adult I carry that same craving to stop and eat here. I loved it as a kid, and I love it now at age 50." Kent Fletcher (Lafayette, IN)

"When I want to indulge in the BEST burger and fries in Minneapolis, I head over here to chow down." Roger Townsend (Bloomington, MN)

"This place just sizzles with grilled ambiance. I love their Plaza Burger." Cynthia Cole (Lafayette, IN)

EATS

Talk of the town

The french fries are hand-cut and hand-blanched. The buns are soft and tasty, the lettuce as if straight from the farmers' market. Nothing frozen, all fresh.

No doubt this place with a stellar reputation is a great place to have lunch. So take an extra-long lunch break; the Convention Grille gets high marks for both food and atmosphere. You can even belly up to the lunch counter and watch your burger get flipped right before your eyes.

Try the Plaza Burger along with homemade chicken noodle soup. In all honesty, the soup made me homesick. And for dessert, indulge in their award-winning hot fudge sundae.

3912 Sunny Side Road (near 42nd Street and France Avenue South)
Edina, MN • 952.920.6881
Open Sun–Thurs 11 a.m.–10 p.m. • Fri & Sat 11 a.m.–11 p.m.

The Elbow Room

Theme for the common man

THE SCOOP The common man's treasure

It's amazing what magic can be found in out-of-the-way places.

Not long ago, a Minneapolis television station conducted a poll to find out where the top ten hamburgers could be found in the state of Minnesota. Many people assumed that the list would be dominated by big city bistros and Lake Country resort dining rooms. Not so.

In the opinion of the people who eat hamburgers everyday, the top ten burgers can be found in a mixed list of taverns, cafés and diners. The word "bistro" never appeared.

One of the "people's choice" for the top ten is the unassuming bar & grill in Albert Lea: The Elbow Room.

This modest-looking building looks more like a house than a public eating and drinking establishment. For 31 years, the focus at The Elbow Room has always centered around the family. Nothing fancy, just a simple, wholesome atmosphere.

EATS Assume nothing

Home-cooked specials include the all-Minnesota favorite: the hot dish. All good food, but of course, the big trophy winner here is the hamburger.

The burger, like the bar, is unassuming. At first glance, it's your basic bar burger until you take your first bite and realize that, indeed, this is magic.

An uncommonly great hamburger found in a common-looking bar deep in the Heartland of America.

The cheeseburger is the real hit at The Elbow Room. For dessert, try the homemade apple streudel.

310 Eighth Street • Albert Lea, MN • 507.373.1836
Open Mon–Fri 7 a.m.–5 p.m. • Sat 7 a.m.–2 p.m.

The Channel Inn

The egg and I

I drove 340 miles for a hamburger at the Channel Inn located on the shoreline of Hall Lake in Fairmont, Minnesota.

Now, this is a unique little burger place.

Perched over the edge of the lake, this log-sided tavern and grill offers two approaches: by land or by water. After all, this is the Land of 10,000 Lakes. It makes perfect sense that boat-loving Minnesotans can call in hamburger orders on cell phones from the middle of the lake, and then cruise over to the dockside take-out window to pick up their food.

Ship to shore. Burger to boat. And there's no limit on your daily catch.

This is a friendly place to linger. In the summertime, the air is infused with onions and beef, sunblock and aloe vera. Take a table out the dock-side eatery and watch the setting sun turn the lake into a chromatic kaleidoscope, and the kids catch minnows with their nets from the dock. It's the perfect place to find complete contentment. A summer utopia.

EATS

Perfect fusion of cluck and beef

Throughout my journey, people I met told me about "this legendary place, somewhere in Minnesota, that puts a fried egg on top of its hamburger."

To be honest, in the grand perspective of the world, this is not a ground-breaking culinary event.

I had a hamburger in Paris with an egg on it. The Danes have a sandwich called a fricadella which employs the same fusion of cluck and beef. But in Minnesota, the land of meat loaf, Jell-O salad and Miracle Whip, this is considered...well, EXOTIC.

Or, put in Minnesota language: "Hey, so, what's the DEAL with this egg thing?"

So dive into the Channel Inn's famous egg-and-burger combination. How does it taste? As slick as moonlight gliding across calm water. As smooth as a glass-covered lake deep in the land of sky blue waters.

330 West Lair Road on Hall Lake • Fairmont, MN • 507.238.9700
Open daily 11 a.m.–8:30 p.m.

Anchor Bar & Grill

All hands on deck

THE SCOOP It is what it is

If Popeye and Olive Oyl owned a bar, this would be it. With a few significant changes...

Popeye wouldn't be eating spinach, and Olive Oyl definitely wouldn't be skinny after eating a regular daily ration of Anchor Burgers and fries.

The ambiance of the place is, well, Old Navy. No, not the clothing store... I mean "Old Navy" as in ore boat models, life vests, portholes, maritime schedules, charts and real sailors knocking back boiler-makers at the bar.

Sailors aren't the only customers here at the Anchor; the daytime crowd attracts a mixture of doctors, lawyers, students and locals.

This is a good place for lunchtime, but here's a hint from an old sailor: Get there early for lunch. The place fills up fast, and by noon time, it's all hands on deck for that prized Anchor Burger.

EATS Full speed ahead burger

The cardiac risk factor at the Anchor is as big as Popeye's bulging forearms. But, hey, this is well worth the risk. The Anchor Burger is an old-fashioned hamburger made with all the juices intact. No skimping here at the Anchor; this is a full-speed-ahead burger.

The french fries are hand cut, like they made them back in the old days. Big fries—finger thick with the skin still on them—stack up like cordwood on the aft deck of your plate.

Check out the photographs and paraphernalia on the walls to catch a glimpse of Lake Superior's shipping history.

If you're really hungry, try a one-pound Galley Burger! If that doesn't anchor your appetite, nothing will.

413 Tower Street • Superior, WI • 715.394.9747
Open daily 11 a.m.–12 a.m.

Deep Water Grill
A deep anchor in historic waters

Once upon a time...

Along the shores of Lake Superior rests a northern port city that is steeped in history and tradition: Ashland, Wisconsin.

Around the turn of the century, Ashland was a boomtown, prosperous by harvesting the riches of natural resources of iron ore and the bountiful timberland that thrived in the hills above the Great Lake. The city flourished with elegant hotels, handsome Victorian homes and stately bank and commerce buildings.

But, times have been cruel to Ashland. Over the last half century, the recovery of mineral and natural resources diminished. The railroad line ceased to exist, leaving the city's great Victorian depot an abandoned architectural orphan—heartless and without a mission.

The changing times took away the old commerce, the old stock and trade. Took away the long ore boats and chugging steam locomotives. Took away the boom and bang of abundant wealth.

But, changing times haven't taken away the spirit and soul of this city.

The great lakeside Victorian hotel has returned. The old beautiful depot is coming back, in spite of a heartbreaking fire. On Main Street, the pulse of commerce is slowly but deliberately coming back. The old red stone buildings of turn-of-the-century elegance are returning to new lives with new missions.

One Main Street building that has taken on a new life is the old Wilmarth's Building. Today, its street-level occupant is the Deep Water Grill and South Shore Brewery. The building has gone through a beautiful restoration. The interior is adorned in amber tones of wood, brick and terra cotta. It is a room filled with cozy booths and ambient light highlighted by an old Victorian back bar imported from St. Louis.

It is the best of the old and the new.

The burger served here is a healthy one; it's big, robust and as tasty as any that I had on my journey. It is best enjoyed in a comfortable atmosphere surrounded by both history and the boom of a new spirit. Besides the Black Angus burger, they are also known for a buffalo brat. Not to be overlooked is the fact that this is a fine microbrewery with a superb selection of beers.

BEEF TIPS

My choice of a companion for that grilled burger is South Shore Brewery's Nut Brown Ale. This restaurant also has a great dessert list. Order an Italian dessert, called a Panacotta, that consists of whipped cream, strawberries, raspberries and blueberries.

808 Main Street West • Ashland, WI • 715.682.4200
Open daily 11 a.m.–10 p.m. dining room •
10:30 p.m.–12 a.m. late–night menu • bar open until 2 a.m.

Digger's Grill & Pizza
Doorway to Hamburger Heaven

The perfect setting

Upon entering this Door County eatery, you are struck by its casual atmosphere punctuated by the sound of laughter. People are having a good time.

To set that light-hearted tone, a small sign reads: "No Shirts, No Ties, No Rednecks." Light and whimsical. Come to think of it, isn't that what we want when we go out to eat? Nothing too serious or too heavy.

People make the case that the hamburger is unhealthy for us. Strictly from an issue of health and diet, they're right.

But, let's not overlook the soul of eating out. It's to enjoy our food in the company of others. Hopefully with people of good cheer equipped with a healthy sense of humor. Call it the Cheeseburger in Paradise spirit. Call it Burger Heaven.

Certainly, it can be found here at Digger's. This is the destination that you "head out to" after a day of golfing, boating or cherry picking in Door County.

At Digger's, eating out means eating OUT. Digger's features an outdoor eating area capped by a cluster of forest green umbrellas. Underneath each umbrella is a row of solar powered lights that look like fireflies hovering over diners on midsummer nights in Door County.

EATS   A memorable meal

The experience of a Door County weekend would not be complete without a memorable meal under those green umbrellas. Dubbed "The Best Burger in Town," one of Digger's famous third-pound Angus burgers with a side of curly fries, or veggies with yogurt dip will do the trick. Other delicious options include the philly cheese steak sandwich, the turkey or ham tourist or a grilled tuna steak. It's enough to make your mouth water.

The signature burger here is Digger's Monster Burger. It's a half-pound two-fisted eating adventure.

4023 Hwy 42 • Fish Creek, WI • 920.868.3095
Open May–Oct 11 a.m.–late

Mitchell's Hilltop Pub & Grill
Point of entry

A barrel of fun

Back in 1955, when the Hilltop was just a 15-barstool tavern, a brief brush with fate granted a legend to this establishment.

The epic tale began when a neighbor made a U-turn in front of the tavern to stop at his mailbox. Unfortunately, a cross-country bus loaded with passengers was speeding along on a collision course with that same U-turning vehicle.

What happened next became an event of split-second timing and fate.

Bernice, the bartender, was cleaning the bar that morning when she heard a baby cry for attention in the room behind the bar. Responding to the baby's cry, she left the bar momentarily to walk into the other room.

Out in front on the highway, the bus driver made a crucial decision. It was either crash into the turning car or take immediate evasive action. He chose the second option and lost control of the bus.

The huge bus careened off the highway, screeched across the tavern parking lot and crashed through the front wall of the Hilltop, smashing into the bar where Bernice had stood. Fortunately, no one was killed. The bus ride left an indelible impression on everyone involved, not to mention the impression it left on the front of the tavern.

Now, nearly a half century later, entry to the Hilltop Bar & Grill is still a unique experience. No, it's not quite as thrilling as riding a speeding bus through the front wall. Today, the port of entry at the Hilltop is a huge door cut in a 100-year-old white oak barrel.

Eight years ago, the owner of the tavern had an opportunity to buy several hand-crafted, century-old German beer vats from the local Point Brewery, which was in the process of converting to stainless steel. The Hilltop selected the best barrel for the doorway of the tavern.

Now what could be more Wisconsin than that? Call it indigenous architecture or just another roadside attraction. In either case, it's a trip worth taking.

And if you come for the barrel, you'll return again and again for the food. The Char-Burgers are seasoned with a secret blend and flame-kissed on an open grill. The Hilltop's famous Friday Fish Fry, served every day, is guaranteed to chase away any Monday blues, even on Tuesday. The Ostrich Burger, found under sandwiches, is low in fat and calories, but high in iron. (Try it and let me know if it tastes like chicken.)

BEEF TIPS

Try their vegetable beef soup with your Char-Burger. Check out the photos on the wall, one taken of the bus and tavern collision of 1955.

4901 Main Street (at Hwy 51 [I-39] and Hwy 10 East) • Stevens Point, WI
715.341.3037 • Open Sun–Wed 10 a.m.–10 p.m. • Thurs–Sat 10 a.m.–11 p.m.

Kroll's East
Titletown burger

So what is it that makes Green Bay so special? Since its population hovers only around 100,000, you probably know more of the people walking down the street here than you would in Milwaukee and Madison. But the phenomenon lies in the numbers of people worldwide connected to this tight-knit community, their hearts swell with pride for the home team: the Green Bay Packers.

This team is the last in the NFL to be community-owned, lending a uniquely strong interest in its success. It's probably why since 1960, every season has been sold out on a season ticket basis, and the waiting list of 60,000 is willing to wait over 30 years for theirs. Ticket holders come from 47 states and D.C. It seems everyone wants to be part of this warm extended family of football fanatics.

The season prompts a family reunion every Sunday (and sometimes Monday). Thus, extraordinary tough love is in the air as the "distant" relatives inevitably emerge, sporting big wigs and Grandma's mumus, cheeseheads and frostbit birthday suits covered in body paint. Hey, everybody's got their special way of supporting the team.

The All-American Family Sunday just wouldn't be complete without good eats. One favorite family pastime is coming in from the cold and enjoying the game with Green Bay's best name in burgers: Kroll's.

THE SCOOP
Another Green Bay legend

In 1936, Kroll's was established by Harry and Caroline Kroll. Initially Kroll's was just a bar, but they began to make their own hamburgers and served sandwiches on toasted semmel rolls.

In 1945 the business was bought by Richard and Isabel Schauer. They reopened as Kroll's BBQ and continued serving hamburgers on semmels for years. Isabel created a chili recipe and added it to the menu along with homemade soups like vegetable, beef and chicken dumpling. The soup and chili became the hallmarks of the restaurant, and remain to this day.

Several of the waitresses at Kroll's East have worked here for over 30 years, which speaks volumes for the longevity of fine service and atmosphere in this small establishment on Green Bay's east side. But, it's not just the friendly ambiance that is striking here. The burger ranks as one of the top five hamburgers that I experienced on my culinary quest.

EATS

High in the ranks

The Kroll's East Cheeseburger is a unique burger that has remained unchanged since its inception in 1936. The meat is still trimmed, ground, seasoned and pressed at the restaurant, so it is always fresh. The cheese is specially blended by a small cheese factory for Kroll's East. The semmel buns are baked at a Quaker bakery every morning. Throw in homemade onion rings and the restaurant's own ketchup mix, and you have an esculent delight befitting the reputation of Titletown.

BEEF TIPS

Kroll's East has spectacular homemade onion rings. And for dessert, try their carrot cake.

658 Main Street • Green Bay, WI • 920.468.4422
Open daily 10:30 a.m.–11 p.m.

Monk's Bar & Grill
The scent of a burger

Grease is the word

Question: How do you draw hungry customers to your establishment?

Well, you could launch a huge ad campaign. Or you could send out buck-a-burger coupons to the locals. Or...

You could position your grill right up front, in the front window with the smell of burgers and fried onions wafting out onto the street.

Monk Heineken, the original owner of the bar called it "aroma marketing." For a half century, burger aficionados have followed their olfactory commands to this place to sit down and indulge in a Monk Burger.

EATS
Sounds and smells of success

This burger is absolutely smothered with onions. But more importantly, it is cooked on an old-fashioned steel grill, gifted with a culinary patina that can only be acquired from years of use. This adds an undeniable (but irresistible) seasoning you'll only find in an old burger joint with the original cooking grill.

Greasy? Oh yeah! But, as every true connoisseur of hamburgers know, grease carries the flavor. Aroma. Flavor. Friendly company inside.

I guess the only intrinsic marketing attraction left to try would be to suspend a microphone over the grill and broadcast the sizzle of a frying Monk Burger down Main Street.

But then again, Monk's Bar & Grill doesn't really need anything! It's already at the top of its game. Just take a whiff at the front door. That scent, folks, is THE SWEET SMELL OF SUCCESS.

BEEF TIPS

For a real challenge, try Monk's Monster Burger.

220 Broadway • Wisconsin Dells, WI • 608.254.2955
Open daily 10 a.m.–11 p.m.

Griff's
All in the family

Some people assume that the best hamburger in the land is the bar burger. Well, remember this is America, and smack dab in the middle of all this great democracy is the American family. One of the most common dinner calls heard in the typical family home sound like this: "Let's eat out tonight."

Many families head out to the national hamburger chains, but some opt for more personal one-of-a-kind grills. More than mom-and-pop royalty, these places have their own signature, personality and warmth. It's the intrinsic human touches that the mega chains sorely lack in favor of robotic efficiency.

Griff's restaurant is a family place.

First, the place is run by a family: the Griffin family. Second, it has a great burger: the Griff Burger. And third, it's in a great location; what could be better than having a good family restaurant perched directly across from a full-service, full-facility, full-tilt city park? This park has all the typical recreation offerings topped with a kite-flying field in the summer and a huge rumbling toboggan and sliding hill when the snow flies.

The perfect solution to feeding a family of different tastes and picky eaters is to present to them the Griff's menu. It's got a full range of items including sandwiches, gyros, Chicago-style hot dogs and great hamburgers, of course. The place is also known for having great broasted chicken.

Try the banana cream pie ice cream cone. After your scrumptious Griff Burger, order cones and take a walk in the park. The best time to do this is on a Sunday afternoon during kite-flying season.

1233 McKenna Boulevard • Madison, WI • 608.276.7466
Open Sat–Thurs 10 a.m.–9 p.m. • Fri 10 a.m.–10 p.m.

The Plaza Tavern
A fine burger at a comfortable level

From all walks of life

This is one of those vintage eateries that defies both the labels of time and the whims of contemporary trends. The Plaza Tavern is a unique entity in the hamburger world.

Opened as a tavern in the 1920s, this terra cotta building is located on a side street in downtown Madison—an address that sets it right between the University of Wisconsin and the State Capitol. This strategic location makes for an interesting mix of students, professors and politicians.

For the past 75 years this diverse clientele has walked through the door at the Plaza and ordered the tavern's classic burger: the Plaza Burger.

EATS Sssssh! It's a secret!

Now, the Plaza Burger's claim to fame is that it comes on a dark rye bun with secret sauce. Yes, secret sauce.

According to one of the locals, it is so secret that a few years ago, several grad students took one of the burgers back to the University lab to break it down and analyze it. As the story goes, they were unsuccessful in decoding and discovering the secret.

It's no secret that it's a great hamburger. According to grill records, it is also a VERY popular burger. By the Plaza's count they have served well over 2.5 million Plaza Burgers since the first patty went on the grill over 70 years ago. This place and its trophy burger has such an acclaimed reputation that I found two other burger hot spots in the Twin Cities that have their own Plaza Burgers on their menu, and have written tributes to the original.

It's obvious when you sit down in one of the Plaza's red vinyl booths that a lot of people have spent time here eating burgers and assembling in good cheer. The booths are so worn and soft that when you sit down you start to slowly sink. By the time the burger arrives, the table top is leveling out at a point somewhere between your chest and your chin.

A new comfort level for the consumption of the American hamburger.

Make no secret about it, the quality and taste of this burger is on a level much higher than the standard franchise hamburger.

BEEF TIPS

Try the Plaza's homemade potato salad to accompany your Plaza Burger.

319 North Henry Street • Madison, WI • 608.255.6592
Open daily 11 a.m.–2 a.m.

The Blue Moon Bar & Grill

Yes Virginia, in Wisconsin, the moon IS made of cheese...

THE SCOOP
Moonbeam

The owners of this urban bar and grill evolved from a great family of restaurant fame and glory.

The Blue Moon Bar & Grill is owned by Larry and Tom Schmock. Their father and mother (Leonard and Janet Schmock) ran Smokey's Steak House in Madison, which several years ago appeared on the cover of Midwest Magazine that championed it as "The Best Steakhouse in the Midwest!"

Well, the fruit doesn't fall far from the tree. The quality and family reputation for fine food and convivial atmosphere continues at the Blue Moon.

EATS
You'll get as full as a harvest moon

But the major departure from Smokey's appears on the menu, for the signature entrée at the Blue Moon is not steak. Rather, it is the Blue Moon Burger (a half pound meat patty topped with bleu cheese and garlic).

For those with larger appetites, there is the half-pound Pile Driver Hamburger—a huge burger topped with ham and three different cheeses, then slathered with fried onions. My goodness, the burgers here are tasty, juicy and as full as a harvest moon.

BEEF TIPS

Try something different with your burger; instead of ordering fries with your sandwich, break from tradition and try chef Doug Reeves' potato salad or cole slaw. His secret recipe for potato salad is so delicious it will render you moonstruck.

2535 University Avenue • Madison, WI • 608.233.0441
Open daily 11 a.m.–2 a.m.

Dotty Dumplings Dowry

Long live the king

A come-from-behind victory

In that vast kingdom of Hamburger Land, is there a true king? Well, the answer is YES, if you ask the people of Madison.

A quarter century ago, Jeff Stanley converted a tiny shoe shine shop to a hamburger stand. The ambiance was eclectic: model airplanes and blimps hung from the ceiling, vintage Kewpie dolls and American Graffiti graphics adorned every square inch of the compact interior of Dotty's.

But a dark shadow encroached upon Dotty's one day. The landlord, a large corporate bank, wanted to tear down Dotty's and build another bank on the site. Even though Jeff had a three-year contract, they wanted Jeff to move. Jeff said NO. The powerful bank replied, "Well, then we will build anyway and excavate around you." So they did; a huge hole was dug around Dotty's.

It was several stories deep. In the center of the ugly pit was a tall butte topped by Dotty's, which had now had a tremendous view. A small, narrow wooden bridge led from the sidewalk across the cavernous abyss to the front door of the hamburger hut. The scene looked like a Disney cartoon. Unstable ground, a treacherous bridge and corporate power...it all looked pretty shaky for Jeff and Dotty's.

But, a funny thing happened on the way to ruin. People recognized Jeff's independent spirit. (Plus he had a great burger!. As the pit went down, Dotty's business went up! Why, even the construction workers who were digging the pit ATE THERE! A pet shop across the street wrote on its storefront marquee, "YOU CAN BANK ON DOTTY'S!"

Well, the bank reconsidered its position and offered Jeff enough money for him to relocate his hamburger business. Jeff Stanley became a local hero, dubbing him "The Hamburger King." His hamburger was consistently voted the best burger in the city for years by public polls. His popularity and credibility for burger royalty was elevated to a national level when USA Today lauded Dotty's as one of the 20 Best Hamburger Establishments in America.

Sounds like a happy ending, but another shadow loomed over his new downtown shop. City hall and powers elite condemned his building in favor of a new municipal building to be constructed on Jeff's site. Offerings of an amount to relocate in downtown Madison were unreasonable for Jeff. So he gave it the good fight; another hole was dug under his place, a series of court rounds ensued, a rousing demonstration of people rallied around Dotty's. But alas, this battle was lost.

Always the champion of the underdog, Jeff Stanley has reopened Dotty Dumplings in downtown Madison. Indeed, the king is back! He's back in business and has reclaimed his kingdom. Long live the king!

I drew Dotty Dumpling herself. She's been the heart and soul of each location, and has stood by Jeff through thick and thin.

EATS
Two-fisted and juicy

The burgers here are two-fisted and juicy. Delicious. This is THE PLACE for lunch in the Capital City. The king himself says, "There's no secret to our hamburger. We just take time to make our burgers and condiments right using fresh ingredients. It's a labor-intensive operation when we assemble these burgers." Believe me when I say it's evident in the first bite.

BEEF TIPS

Dotty's has a fantastic menu. Jeff did have one bit of advice: "Always have a touch of pink in your burger." And my advice: Order the fudge-bottom pie, their signature dessert.

317 North Frances Street • Madison, WI • 608.259.0000
Open daily 11 a.m.–1 a.m.

Grumpy Troll Brew Pub & Restaurant

Let the good times troll

THE SCOOP

Don't let the name fool you. This is not a grumpy place.

On the contrary, enter the door at the Grumpy Troll and you step into an environment of laughter and good cheer. Its warm interior of oak booths and soft ambient light is always filled with friendly people in the blissful pursuit of the enjoyment of life.

There's not a grump in sight.

The Grumpy Troll is in Mt. Horeb, a hill-hugging community nestled in the driftless region of southwestern Wisconsin. Deeply rooted in Norwegian heritage, this town carries a Scandinavian charm with patriotic pride. One can see it in the festivals, culture and local architecture.

Part of this enchantment is its folklore. The revolving metaphor of stories about the troll is prominent in Norwegian folklore and legend. Under the bridge, in the forest, down by the river...he's always there.

Like Shakespeare's Puck.

In Mt. Horeb, you see him everywhere. Much like the dragon in China, the troll has become the mascot and local icon of Mt. Horeb. His likeness is carved in wood along Main Street. There is a flag flying with his image emblazoned upon it.

EATS

A bit of a misnomer

This is a microbrewery which has local beers. My suggestion is to order a sampler ring of the beer offerings to catch the local flavor that suits your palate best. My favorite was How Now Brown Cow.

Mt. Horeb is the home of the National Mustard Museum, just two blocks from the Grumpy Troll. It is well worth the visit.

So, of course, when you enter this microbrewery/eatery, a Troll Burger is a suggested burger, which comes with a side order of Grumpy Chips. Or, try the Skogstroll, which is a hamburger named after a wild mushroom-eating troll of the North Woods.

Be forwarned that in the process of eating this delicious Black Angus delight...it's next to impossible to fall into a grumpy mood. So let the good times troll.

105 South Second Street • Mount Horeb, WI • 608.437.BREW
Open Mon–Sat 11 a.m.–10 p.m. • Sun 10 a.m.–10 p.m.

American Legion Burger Stand

Small wonder

It was obvious from the beginning of this quest that the hamburger can be found in establishments of all shapes, sizes and locations: stainless steel diners, smoky taverns, country clubs and 1950s-style drive-ins. All separate identities, yet they have the same common denominator—they all serve up their own local variation of the great American hamburger.

THE SCOOP

Small place, big heart

Certainly the smallest hamburger establishment that I came across was the American Legion Post 67 Hamburger Stand in Lake Mills, Wisconsin.

This place is so small that there is no room to eat inside. Patrons line up at the sidewalk window to order their hamburgers. It is the definitive take-out place. It's a burger stand with the basics: a door, a window, and a great hamburger, proving that American legends come in all sizes.

How popular is the burger? Popular enough to have a football bowl game named after it! Several years ago, the two high schools in town made a friendly bet. When they met in the annual cross-town rivalry football game, the team that lost would buy the other team hamburgers—sliders from the Legion Hamburger Stand. So sports buffs and burger buffs coined the title game "The Sliderbowl."

EATS

It's magic

It's your basic hamburger, bun and fixings. But the draw is legendary; this burger stand has such a strong reputation, word-of-mouth from as far away as Madison brought me here. If it's good enough that people from Madison are recommending it before all the grills in their big city, it's gotta be worth the trip.

How does one explain this journey beyond the big city limits for something as everyday ordinary as a hamburger? It's magic.

Not so at Joseph Megaan's. The Buffalo Burger that Tom cooked for us was as good as any that I had out West.

Isn't it fitting? Here's a town that spawned a great entrepreneur of a famous Western stagecoach line. Today, this prairie town has two creative individuals with that same entrepreneurial spirit fostering an appreciation of history along with the contemporary elegance of fine dining and lodging.

Now, that's what I call dancing back the buffalo with grace and style.

BEEF TIPS

After your Buffalo Burger, splurge a little on the blueberry strawberry cream cheese pie.

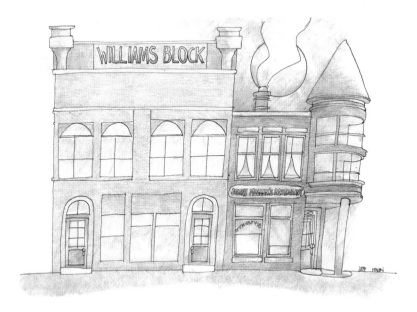

101 Main Street South • Lake Mills, WI • 920.648.3005
Open Mon–Fri 11 a.m.–9 p.m. • Sat 7:30 a.m.–9:30 p.m. • Sun 8 a.m.–9 p.m.

Pete's Hamburger Stand

For Pete's sake, keep it simple

Semi-ancient tradition

One creative contribution to the burger world goes way back to 1909, when a local entrepreneur named Pete Gorky started his hamburger business with an umbrella pushcart. He traveled around to fairs, festivals and carnivals serving his burgers.

Over the years, Pete's cart evolved into this sidewalk stand.

It has remained a family operation all those years. Over four generations of family members have been flipping burgers and working the window.

The tradition continues today, closing in on 100 years of simple magic.

EATS   Something's in the water

Now this is getting back to the basics. How basic?

There is no menu at this little Main Street hamburger stand. There is only one food item that you can order: a hamburger. No cheese. No pickles. No lettuce and tomato. In fact, you have only one decision to make: with onions or without.

Simple. No frills.

In this day of gourmet twenty-five dollar burgers, this simplicity may seem like a detriment. But bite into one of these streetwise hamburgers and you will realize, "NO! Nothing is missing! This is a great-tasting hamburger! What's the secret?"

Again, it's a simple answer. It's water! The burgers are covered with an inch of water and cooked in a stainless steel pan over gas burners. The reward of this simple process is a delicious hamburger.

The only decision is with or without onions. So unless you're on a date, don't turn down onions!

118 West Blackhawk Avenue (across from Stark's Sporting Goods)
Prairie Du Chien, WI • 608.326.6653 • Open May–Oct Fri–Sun 11 a.m.–9 p.m.

Solly's Grille
Dairyland delight

They kept coming back for more

One afternoon, I took a seat at Solly's front counter next to a happy-looking senior couple who appeared to know the territory at this home-like eatery on Milwaukee's north side. It was obvious that they were regular customers of the place.

"How long have you been coming here?" I inquired.

"A long time," they replied.

"How long is that?" I asked.

"Oh...let me think a moment. Harriet, when did we have our first hamburger here?"

"It was 1944 or 1945, Richard."

1945! My goodness, I thought. These people have been eating here for 57 years!

"It's really not that rare," owner Glen Salmon informed me. "We have people eating here who started with us when we opened back in 1936. We have a nice mix of seniors, students, television anchormen, major league sports figures, professional people and blue-collar folks. It's a harmonious community in itself.

"Bob Uecker has eaten here for so long that we put a little brass name tag on his favorite bar stool, honoring 25 years of his humor and eating our hamburgers."

EATS   The pride of Wisconsin

"So," I asked, "what's the secret that attracts all this loyalty to one particular grill in Suds City?"

"We are a family-owned operation," Glen replied. "We use fresh beef, along with an age-old recipe that involves A LOT OF BUTTER."

Butter literally drips down your chin when you eat a burger here.

Glen showed me a brick of butter next to the sizzling grill. "We go through 120 pounds of butter a week making our hamburgers and cheeseburgers."

Butter. Cheese. Well, this is Dairyland, and there is a national reputation to uphold. I can't think of a more delicious way to ensure our state's namesake than to sit on a counter stool at Solly's and chomp on a butter-dripping hamburger.

"On Wisconsin!" I said, "And while you're at it, I'll take another cheese-burger to go."

BEEF TIPS

Wash everything down with a chocolate banana malt served in a cool, steel cup. It's a house favorite.

4629 North Port Washington Road • Glendale, WI • 414.332.8808
Open Tues–Sat 6:30 a.m.–8 p.m.

Bella's Fat Cat Café

The cat's meow

To outsiders, Milwaukee appears to be the city that beer made famous. Suds city, Brewtown, Brewskyville...

That's true to a point, but that's not all this city is famous for.

For those who really know Milwaukee know that THIS IS THE PLACE to find an incredible array of frozen custard stands unlike any other in the land. Forget Brewtown, this is Custard City!

That fine reputation of great frozen concoction is abundantly apparent in this tiny storefront burger and custard stand found on Milwaukee's north side.

THE SCOOP   What's in a name?

For years, owner Michael Schmidt worked for a large custard chain in the city. But you see, Michael's the kind of guy who has an independent spirit. Several years ago, he struck out on his own and looked at starting his own business. He experimented with a bar/night club venture before settling on this hamburger and custard café on Brady Street. But he needed a name for his new business.

One night at home while brainstorming for an idea, his cat jumped into his lap of imagination. There it was right in front of him! Bella, his cat, who just happened to be fat.

Now, for the uninitiated, the Brady Street neighborhood is a hip community of intelligent souls who can recognize a good thing at the drop of a hat. When Michael put up his sign, people flocked through the doors, even before construction was finished.

The word quickly spread that Mike and his staff grilled a tremendous hamburger and made fabulous malts and custards in over 60 flavors!

Yes, I did say 60.

But be forewarned; if you become a regular customer at Bella's, where the burgers are big and the custard is heavenly, you could become a fat cat yourself! FAT and HAPPY.

BEEF TIPS

You can customize your burgers at Bella's. My suggestion is to order one with Bella Sauce.

The custard flavor changes by the day. (Custard Diem!) On the day we dined at Bella's, we were fortunate to have ordered Tiramisu Custard. Believe me...it was the cat's meow!

1233 East Brady Street • Milwaukee, WI • 414.273.2113
Open daily 11 a.m.–11 p.m.

The Shanti Bar & Grill

It's a Gunder-ful life

Several times during my journey I heard the story of a legendary hamburger that can only be found in Iowa.

Like Paul Bunyan, the tale grew as I traveled across the Heartland and heard accounts of its existence. Comments like, "The biggest burger I ever ate," "A great burger large enough to feed a family of four," and "Best burger I ever had in my life!" freely came my way.

Even one of my doctors in Madison let slip this unhealthy advice: "You haven't experienced a hamburger until you've had a GUNDERBURGER!"

So it came to pass, on a gray day in early spring that I started out on a 300-mile quest to find the Gunderburger.

Just west of Dubuque, I found it. The small burg of Gunder, Iowa, sits atop a driftless ridge in a rolling landscape befitting of a Grant Wood painting. A small collection of houses and farm buildings, Gunder has only one commercial enterprise: a small tavern called the Shanti.

The tavern is located on Gunder Road (of course), and is the home of the largest burger that I've viewed in captivity.

The Gunderburger weighs in at a pound and a half. How big? Big enough to fit over the cover of my sketchbook. Big enough to make the conventional-sized bun look like a small bottle cap surrounded by Iowa beef. And tasty enough to be chosen "One of the Top 21 Hamburgers in America" by the National Cattlemen's Beef Association in 1996.

How widespread is its reputation? Well, the little town has a population of 28. On a typical day in Gunder, the little roadside tavern goes through a hundred pounds of beef!

Try that on for size.

Sure, you could make your way to the Shanti by yourself. But, good luck trying to finish your burger! Make this one a group activity; the giant Gunderburger will feed several people. Do as the locals and ask your waitress for Country Bob's BBQ Sauce. Then satisfy your sweet tooth with Dutch apple pie, that is, if you have room.

17455 Gunder Road • Gunder, IA • 563.864.9289
Open Mon–Sat 11 a.m.–10 p.m.

Kalmes Restaurant
Iowa basics

Charm, comfort and convenience

At day's end on the open road, the complexities of travel fade away to simple needs: a place to eat and sleep.

The basics of life.

Well, everything about this small Iowa town is basic. There are just two businesses in town: a delightful historic inn and a wonderful restaurant directly across the highway. Charm, comfort and convenience.

The inn is a beautifully restored 1850 roadhouse, offering bed & breakfast hospitality. The lineage in St. Donatus reaches back to early settlers who immigrated here from Luxembourg. The architecture and the look of the village echoes that European influence. St. Donatus feels and looks very much like a small roadside hamlet in the old country.

Across the street, Kalmes Restaurant exudes an atmosphere of that European charm mixed with the spice and character of rural Iowa. The night that I stopped to eat here, the restaurant was filled with happy diners following that basic mission of life to eat, drink and be merry.

Vintage Patsy Cline and Hank Williams, Sr. wafted out of the jukebox. This is a people place. Friendly and engaging. An assortment of farmers, truckers and tourists dined in warm comraderie.

EATS Amazing grace

Kalmes offers a full menu featuring prime rib, homemade chicken soup and a hamburger that ranks right up there with the best in the Midwest.

As I chomped down on my burger, I looked up at the plaque above my table. It read, "Iowa Restaurant of the Year 2001." What a revelation to realize; in the smallest of places, a traveling wayfarer can find amazing graces.

You won't find this just anywhere: get the Olive Burger, a.k.a. the "I Love You" Burger, topped with sliced green olives and swiss cheese. And try their chicken noodle soup, made with homemade noodles.

100 North Main Street • St. Donatus, IA • 563.773.2480
Open Mon–Sat 7:30 a.m.–9 p.m. • Sun 7:30 a.m.–8 p.m.

The Hamburg Inn

Presidential approval

All hail

If there was a theme song associated with this hamburger spot, most likely it would be "Hail to the Chief."

Both President Ronald Reagan and President Bill Clinton have chowed down at this unassuming hamburger parlor located in the Heartland of America. This is a hamburger spot that receives not only presidential approval, but also garners rave reviews from the locals. Of course, this nationally-renowned reputation did not come overnight.

It stretches back to the mid-1930s when Joe Panther first opened the Hamburg Inn. Later, his brother Adrian came on board as a partner. Over the years, the restaurant grew through family ownership and became a small chain with three locations.

Quality burgers and family charm have always reigned as the common denominators in each of the Hamburg Inns in Iowa City. Today only one shop remains: the Number 2 shop located on Iowa Avenue, a few blocks from the University of Iowa. A proud survivor.

The Hamburg Inn has received national acclaim from the Washington Post, NPR's All Things Considered and the New York Times. The Inn is also repeatedly mentioned in America's Best Eats guide books. With good reason, the hamburgers here are made with loving care.

EATS   Quality, freshness, time & effort

Made with fresh daily ground chuck, the burgers are hand-patted with emphasis on quality and freshness. Time and effort that produces a wonderful burger.

Chow down at the Hamburg Inn and that theme song would likely have a new title: "Hail to the Chef."

For a variation, try the Hula Burger: an exotic burger covered with swiss cheese and pineapple. If you're here early, try one of the Inn's 60 different egg omelets.

214 North Linn Street • Iowa City, IA • 319.337.5512
Open daily 6 a.m.–11 p.m.

Taylor's Maid-Rite
Ketchup rules!

The 11th Commandment

The red-lettered sign at Taylor's was clear and simple. It read: NO KETCHUP.

The questioned begged to be asked. Why?

The grill master at Taylor's offered up this story: "Back in the 1930s, the original owner of Taylor's, Cliff Taylor, noticed that the town hobos would frequent the hamburger establishment and spirit away the ketchup packets at the counter. They would bring the ketchup back to their camp and add them to boiling water to make tomato soup. Cliff decided to put an end to that practice, so he issued the commandment that still stands today: NO KETCHUP."

"Yes," I replied, "but that was over 70 years ago." Hobos are an endangered species and certainly the few that still ride the rails have evolved to desire more contemporary cuisines at their campfires. "Why is the sign and rule still in existence?"

"Well, the original owner was so insistent on the no ketchup law that he included it as a part of the terms of sale when he sold his hamburger business to the new owners."

Be forewarned that when you sit down at this little burger stop: THOU SHALT NOT CONSUME KETCHUP.

EATS Angle of attack

Taylor's is one of the original Maid-Rite hamburger establishments in America. The chain started in 1929 and has become a legend, first in Iowa and now across the land.

The burger is a classic loose beef Iowa hamburger cooked on a diagonal grill that allows the grease to drip down, following the slant to the grill.

On the way to Taylor's, I was advised by a local farmer to ask for my hamburger to be WET. The distinction is that the hamburger meat near the bottom of the slanted grill is juicier and more favorable. (Conversely, the higher meat is a dry burger.) Having tried both I'm INCLINED to agree with that wise farmer from Iowa.

(BEEF TIPS)

For dessert, ask for a thick slice of cherry pie à la mode.

106 South Third Avenue • Marshalltown, IA • 641.753.9684
Open Mon–Sat 8 a.m.–10 p.m. • Sun 10 a.m.–10 p.m.

Maxie's
Happy Max

I've traveled a lot, not just searching for hamburgers, but simply for the sake of traveling. Call it a gypsy soul. Big cities and small towns, from Peking to Park Rapids.

In my travels, I've dined at some great restaurants and cafés across the world. Great food with exotic locations. The other night, when I walked into this restaurant on the west side of Des Moines, I walked into a dining experience that I could only describe as a MAXIMUM dining pleasure.

THE SCOOP
With a side of bliss

This city's famous burger is called "The Maxie": a half-pound hamburger that's been around for over 25 years garnering plaudits and praise of legendary status and stature.

It's a great burger that lives up to its state-wide reputation, but, I found something else that doesn't appear on the menu. Something that appeals to the hunger of the human spirit. This is a happy place.

It's obvious from the laughter and cheer exchanged between Jim, his staff and the diner that the magic here is not just found on the plate. It's found in the upbeat attitude and atmosphere that permeates the interior of this fine restaurant. Intrinsic elements of bliss and joy served up freely with your juicy burger.

EATS
Pizzaz in burger eating

The giant Maxie is surrounded by a mound of steaming onion rings. Now, the onion rings are a story in their own right. Great care is applied to choosing the right onions—sweet onions from Texas—that are hand-peeled and prepared the proper way.

When my Maxie came out to the table, owner Jim Glenn gave me some culinary advice: "Stick that sweet onion right on your burger, not fried, but raw. It's the pizzaz in burger eating that many people miss." This is comfort food to the max.

The Maxie Burger is the signature menu offering. Order it with onion rings and be sure to try Maxie's bread pudding, which arrives on a huge plate surrounded by scoops of whipped cream and ice cream. Delicious!

1311 Grand Avenue • West Des Moines, IA • 515.223.1463
Open Mon–Thurs 11 a.m.–2 p.m. & 5 p.m.–9:30 p.m.
Fri 11 a.m.–2 p.m. & 5 p.m.–10:30 p.m. • Sat 4:30 p.m.–10:30 p.m.

Stella's Hamburgers

Getting to know Stella

The dining experience has an added dimension of quality when the relationship between owner and customer evolves from a mutual appreciation for one another into unique friendship. It's good to know that your order is prepared with tender-loving care by a good friend. Stella and Al are two such owners you want to befriend.

Although she died in 1985, Stella Sullivan is the spirit that continues to work magic through her son, Al. When Al and I spoke, I got to know Stella, and found the same endearing qualities in him as well.

True, this Stella's is in Omaha, Nebraska, and technically outside the geographic realm of this book. But, Stella's has been writing a history of food that is out of this world. Known as a Nebraska landmark, it's definitely a must-stop when you're just across the river in Council Bluffs, Iowa.

THE SCOOP
She's a gem

Al took over Stella's in 1974 when Stella had a stroke. He said this of his mother: "Stella was a very strong, independent, hard-working woman. "She had to take care of my three sisters and me after my dad passed away when I was one."

But they all helped with the business. What started as a bar in one of the rooms of the Sullivans' three-room house, Stella's then started serving sandwiches. As the business grew they added a grill to serve burgers and later moved to a new building in 1949. Al said, "Ma remembered that day well because it was Friday, the 13th of May."

It may have been their lucky strike.

EATS
Famous fries

You'll make a connection with Stella through the locals that have dined here since she was in charge: "If you think the food is good now, you should have tasted it when Stella cooked!"

Stella's serves locals and visitors alike, but with one stipulation: you HAVE to be a french fry lover. You may have forgotten that fries are made of potatoes, until you've encountered Stella's objects of perfection, hand-cut and made fresh. In the summertime, Al cuts up over 1,000 pounds of potatoes a week!

The fries come in a bowl and the burgers on a napkin. The burgers are huge, mouthwatering and cheap. And simply divine.

BEEF TIPS

Get cheese and grilled onions atop your Stella Burger, accompanied by a bowl of fries. Be sure to say hi to Al too.

106 Galvin Road South • Bellevue, NE • 402.291.6088
Open Mon–Fri 11 a.m.–8 p.m. • Sat 11 a.m.–3 p.m.

Hamburger Hall of Fame
The grill of victory

The story goes that this little town called Seymour in northeastern Wisconsin is the birthplace of the hamburger sandwich.

To add to the tale, it was invented by a teenager!

Seymour's alleged claim to fame dates back to a hot day in 1885, when a young fifteen-year-old named Charlie Nagreen came to the Seymour Outagamie County Fair in an ox-drawn wagon. As the locals relate, young Charlie opened his stand to sell meatballs to fair-goers.

Well, strolling fair patrons were just not interested in stopping to eat meatballs.

So, you might say that meatball sales went flat. Charlie, in a desperate moment, had a bolt of inspiration. He flattened the meatballs, placed the meat between two pieces of bread and voilà! Customers could TAKE OUT their meals to eat while they strolled along the sawdust lanes of the fairgrounds.

Charlie called the creation a "hamburger." He became a popular attraction at the annual fair for the next 65 years. People came for his delicious hamburger (which were fried in butter—ON WISCONSIN!) and to meet the legendary Hamburger Charlie. He continues to be a legend, even after he passed away in 1951.

Other towns across the country have laid claim to the hamburger invention and it's a matter of conjecture. But the locals fervently defend Charlie and his original creation—the fairgrounds hamburger—that forever changed American eating habits.

Charlie became the town's pride, and to champion that, Seymour created the Hamburger Hall of Fame. The Hamburger Hall of Fame displays artifacts, paraphernalia, records and books referencing the history of the hamburger in America.

Seymour celebrates their Burger Fest with a giant parade, entertainment, a run, a ketchup slide competition and occasionally a crack at cooking the largest burger on Earth.

To accomplish that task, the town built the world's largest hamburger grill: a mega grill that in 1989 broke the Guinness World Record for the largest hamburger weighing 5,520 pounds! It was large enough to serve 13,000 hungry festival visitors.

The whole town gets into the act during Burger Fest, which is held annually on the first Saturday in August.

126 North Main Street • Seymour, WI 54165 • 920.833.9522

White Castle
Midnight Slyder

I grew up on White Castle hamburgers. As a kid, our family bought them by the sackful. Later, during my college years, White Castle was the only place open in the middle of the night or during deep-winter blizzards.

All those times when I ate six, eight or ten of them, I was totally unaware of the historic role that the White Castle chain played in the building of the American Hamburger Dynasty. Let's delve into the influence that the White Castle had on the hamburger. We'll call it Hamburger History 101.

To begin, the White Castle was the first hamburger chain in America. Nearly a half century before McDonald's in 1916, an entrepreneur in Kansas City named J. Walter Anderson came up with an idea to flatten beef and shredded onions into small patties. Then the beef was seared at high temperature on both sides, effectively sealing in the juices of the hamburger.

Anderson also came up with the hamburger bun. Before he came along, hamburgers were served between two pieces of bread. Anderson had a bakery make special buns and then placed them on top of the cooking hamburger to absorb the flavor of the meat and shredded onions.

Soon, people were flocking to the little hamburger stand. In 1920, J. Walter opened two more stands, starting a chain. He and his new partner, Edgar Waldo Ingram, opened their fourth location with a distinctive style of architecture. It was to become its signature: a white castle to symbolize cleanliness, purity and security. The shape was inspired by the Chicago water tower which mimics a classic medieval castle.

The little burger—sold for a nickel—took off and soon the hamburger stands were spreading across the land. The public could recognize and rely upon its standardized format and distinctive architecture. By 1930, well over 100 White Castles were in operation across ten states.

In addition, White Castle was the first business to advertise hamburgers in the newspaper. One ad included a $1 coupon that could be clipped and redeemed for a sackful of 20 burgers! The ad campaign was so successful that the company had to create a special container for the hamburgers: a small castle-like carton with a fitted partition to prevent the hamburgers from getting squashed in the bag.

In the mid-1950s, the standard White Castle burger was slightly modified by using holes in the meat patties. This allowed the burger to cook quicker and the heat to penetrate the patty, while steaming the bun at the same time.

This little 1921 White Castle that I drew represents all those Castle grills that dot the urban landscape. When I see them late at night, I am reminded of that beautiful oil painting Nighthawks painted by Edward Hopper—a small nocturnal population gathered together on stainless steel barstools in shiny white tile buildings, etched in the middle of the indigo night.

Burger Wisconsin

Meanwhile, on the other side of the world...

Meanwhile, on the other side of the world in New Zealand, there exists an American oasis—a '50s style "burger bar" (as the Kiwis would say) called Burger Wisconsin. Americans traveling through Auckland have rated this burger as the best in town, but not for its close resemblance to a burger from the states. The Kiwis have added their own twists; two bun halves sandwich endless permutations of ingredients including—but not limited to—avocado, ginger, cranberry or apricot sauce, garlic, honey, cream cheese, venison and relish.

So be proud, Wisconsin, for even on opposite ends of the globe, the state has a pervasive reputation for a supreme taste in burgers. And well-representing your country, without your knowledge, is still well-representing your country.

Here's a menu from the Burger Wisconsin chain. See how New Zealand has made the greatness of the all–American one they can call their own:

burger WISCONSIN

Lunch 12-2pm 7 days; Dinner Sun-Thur 5-8.30pm;
Fri & Sat 5-9.00pm.

Phone orders welcome - Prices are subject to change

① **Basic:** -1/4 lb Prime beef, salad & relish		$4.90
② **Cheese:** -1/4 lb Prime beef, melted cheese, salad & relish		$5.70
③ **Pestarella:** -1/4 lb Prime beef, pesto & mozzarella cheese, salad & relish		$7.00
④ **Venison:** -1/4 lb Marinated venison strips, salad & relish		$8.90
⑤ **Camembert:** -1/4 lb Prime beef, camembert, salad & relish		$6.50
⑥ **Blue Cheese:** -1/4 lb Prime beef, blue cheese dressing, salad & relish		$5.90
⑦ **Chicken:** -Chicken breast, salad & relish		$7.40
⑧ **Chicken Cream Cheese & Apricot:** -Chicken breast, cream cheese & herbed apricot sauce-salad		$8.90
⑨ **Chilli:** -1/4 lb Prime Beef, chilli sauce, salad & relish		$5.70
⑩ **Black Pepper:** -1/4 lb Prime beef, coated in peppercorns, salad & relish		$5.40
⑪ **Sour Cream:** -1/4 lb Prime beef, sour cream, salad & relish		$5.90
⑫ **Jamaican:** -1/4 lb Prime beef, honey & ginger sauce, salad & relish		$6.20
⑬ **Satay:** -1/4 lb Prime beef, satay sauce, salad & relish		$5.90
⑭ **Garlic Mayo:** -1/4 lb Prime beef, garlic, mayonnaise, salad & relish		$5.90
⑮ **Vegetarian:** -Soya bean, sesame seed pattie, salad & relish		$5.90
⑯ **Chicken Camembert & Cranberry:** -Chicken breast, camembert & cranberry sauce, salad		$8.90
⑰ **Junior Burger:** -Small unseasoned burger, cheese, tomato sauce		$3.50
⑱ **Avocado Bacon:** -1/4 lb Prime beef, avocado & bacon, salad & relish		$7.20
⑲ **Avocado Bacon & Chicken:** -Chicken breast, avocado & bacon, salad & relish		$9.20

EXTRAS: -Combine ingredients from our menu to make your own delicious burger; Fries $2.00;
Sauces (blue cheese, garlic mayo, sour cream, chilli, satay, relish, mayonnaise) $1.00; Shakes $2.00.

10 Shakespeare Rd, Napier: **Phone 835 9615**

ring (04) 568 9050

For any information regarding Wisconsin franchises

The Trail's End

Notes from a cabin in the North

Here I am at journey's end, taking time to reflect on this long quest to find the Holy Grill. I pulled off the road for the night, rented a small cabin from a friendly family, and decided to reflect on what I've learned about hamburgers and people this past year.

I've found a place to relax on a porch swing, and I'm looking up at a big moon rising up over bone-white birch trees. Time has stalled out over this small cabin in the North. The perspective of my journey has become clear and absolute.

I had set out to find THE Holy Grill. What I found is that there is no SINGULAR Holy Grill. Looking up at the stars, I have realized that there is a multitude of Holy Grills, as vast as the stars above.

Many of the people I met and interviewed have claimed that the Holy Grill is a shrine in their backyard in the form of wrought iron and aluminum. They fire up their grills and conduct their own communal rituals in the comforts of backyard kingdoms. I understand that.

I appreciate the fact that one does not need to journey far to find their own personal Holy Grill. Stepping out on the back porch is far enough to capture the sizzle and flavor of that perfect hamburger.

I have one suggestion for you: whether your preference is a roadside restaurant or your backyard, I've found that the perfect condiment for any hamburger is laughter. It's the intrinsic spice of life that is served up best in the company of friends. There is nothing better than friends sharing the enjoyment of the perfect burger on a perfect night.

Follow your bliss and savor the moment that will truly make your grill a sacred place to be.

Jeff Hagen

Where's the Beef?

Minnesota's Holy Grills

Andy's Garage 1825 University Avenue • St. Paul, MN
651.917.2332 • Open Mon–Thurs 7 a.m.–8 p.m. • Fri & Sat 7 a.m.–10 p.m.

The Channel Inn 330 West Lair Road on Hall Lake • Fairmont, MN
507.238.9700 • Open daily 11 a.m.–8:30 p.m.

The Convention Grille 3912 Sunny Side Road • Edina, MN
952.920.6881 • Open Sun–Thurs 11 a.m.–10 p.m. • Fri & Sat 11 a.m.–11 p.m.

Elbow Room 310 Eighth Street • Albert Lea, MN
507.373.1836 • Open Mon–Fri 7 a.m.–5 p.m. • Sat 7 a.m.–2 p.m.

Gordy's Hi Hat 415 Sunnyside Drive • Cloquet, MN 55720
218.879.6125 • Open mid-March–first week of Oct 10 a.m.–9 p.m.
(or until the last customer leaves)

The Hi Ho Tavern 10 Center Avenue East • Dilworth, MN
218.287.2975 • Open Sat–Thurs 11 a.m.–10 p.m. • Fri 11 a.m.–11 p.m.

Lion's Tap 16180 Flying Cloud Drive • Eden Prairie, MN • 952.934.5299
Open Mon–Thurs & Sun 11 a.m.–10 p.m. • Fri & Sat 11 a.m.–11 p.m.

Lockport Marketplace & Deli 5362 West Hwy 61 • Lutsen, MN •
218.663.7548 • Open daily 7 a.m.–10 p.m.

Matt's Bar 3500 Cedar Avenue South • Minneapolis, MN
612.729.9936 Open Mon–Wed 11 a.m.–12 a.m. • Thurs–Sat 11 a.m.–1 a.m.
Sun 12 p.m.–12 a.m.

Mickey's Diner 36 West Seventh Street • Downtown, St. Paul, MN
651.222.5633 • Open 24 hours a day • 7 days a week

My Sister's Place 410 East Hwy 61 (P.O. Box 248) • Grand Marais, MN
218.387.1915 • Open Sun–Thurs 11 a.m.–9 p.m. • Fri & Sat 11 a.m.–10 p.m.

The Nook 492 Hamline Avenue South • St. Paul, MN
651.698.4347 • Open Sun–Thurs 10 a.m.–10 p.m. • Fri & Sat 10 a.m.–11 p.m.

Ray's Grill & the North Pole Bar 5610 Raleigh Street • Duluth, MN
218.628.1865 • Open Mon–Sat 8 a.m.–2 p.m.

Snuffy's Malt Shop 244 South Cleveland Avenue • Highland Park, MN
651.690.1846 • Open Mon–Sat 11 a.m.–9 p.m. • Sun 12 p.m.–9 p.m.

Whitey's Café 121 DeMers Avenue • East Grand Forks, MN
218.773.1831 • Open daily 11 a.m.–10 p.m. • bar menu 10 p.m.–12 a.m.

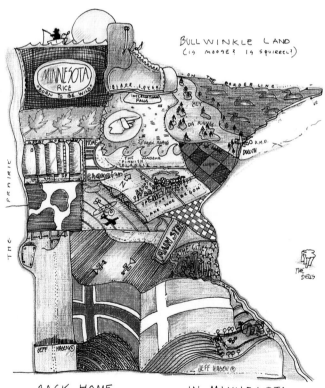

BACK HOME.   IN MINNESOTA

Where's the Beef?
Wisconsin's Holy Grills

Anchor Bar & Grill 413 Tower Street • Superior, WI
715.394.9747 • Open daily 11 a.m.–12 a.m.

Bella's Fat Cat Café 1233 East Brady Street • Milwaukee, WI
414.273.2113 • Open daily 11 a.m.–11 p.m.

The Blue Moon Bar & Grill 2535 University Avenue • Madison, WI
608.233.0441 • Open daily 11 a.m.–2 a.m.

Deep Water Grill 808 Main Street West • Ashland, WI • 715.682.4200
Open daily 11 a.m.–10 p.m. • late-night menu 10:30 p.m.–12 a.m.

Dotty Dumplings 317 North Frances Street • Madison, WI
608.259.0000 • Open daily 11 a.m.–1 a.m.

Griff's 1233 McKenna Boulevard • Madison, WI
608.276.7466 • Open Sat–Thurs 10 a.m.–9 p.m. • Fri 10 a.m.–10 p.m.

Grumpy Troll Brew Pub & Restaurant 105 South Second Street
Mount Horeb, WI • 608.437.BREW • Open Mon–Sat 11 a.m.–10 p.m.
Sun 10 a.m.–10 p.m.

Joseph Megaan's Restaurant & Pub 101 Main Street South
Lake Mills, WI • 920.648.3005 • Open Mon–Fri 11 a.m.–9 p.m.
Sat 7:30 a.m.–9:30 p.m. • Sun 8 a.m.–9 p.m.

Kroll's East 1658 Main Street • Green Bay, WI 54302
920.468.4422 • Open daily 10:30 a.m.–11 p.m.

American Legion Burger Stand 133 North Main Street • Lake Mills, WI
920.648.3460 • Open May–Oct on Fridays • call ahead for hours

Mitchell's Hilltop Pub & Grill 4901 Main Street • Stevens Point, WI
715.341.3037 • Open Sun–Wed 10 a.m.–10 p.m. • Thurs–Sat 10 a.m.–11 p.m.

Monk's Bar & Grill 220 Broadway • Wisconsin Dells, WI
608.254.2955 • Open daily 10 a.m.–11 p.m.

Pete's Hamburger Stand 118 West Blackhawk Street
Prairie Du Chien, WI • Open May–October Fri–Sun 11 a.m.–9 p.m.

The Plaza Tavern 319 North Henry Street • Madison, WI
608.255.6592 Open daily 11 a.m.–2 a.m.

Solly's Grille 4629 North Port Washington Road • Glendale, WI
414.332.8808 • Open Tues–Sat 6:30 a.m.–8 p.m.

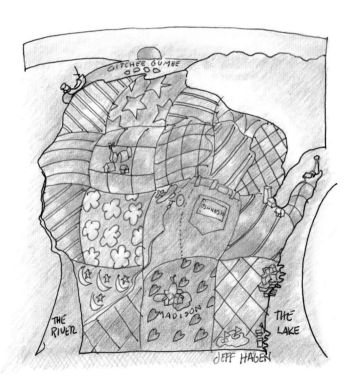

Where's the Beef?
Iowa's Holy Grills

The Hamburg Inn 214 North Linn Street • Iowa City, IA
319.337.5512 • Open daily 6 a.m.–11 p.m.

Kalmes Restaurant 100 North Main Street • St. Donatus, IA
563.773.2480 • Open Mon–Sat 7:30 a.m.–9 p.m. • Sun 7:30 a.m.–8 p.m.

Maxie's 1311 Grand Avenue • West Des Moines, IA •
515.223.1463 • Open Mon–Thurs 11 a.m.–2 p.m. & 5 p.m.–9:30 p.m.
Fri 11 a.m.–2 p.m. & 5 p.m.–10:30 p.m. • Sat 4:30 p.m.–10:30 p.m.

The Shanti Bar & Grill 17455 Gunder Road • Gunder, IA
563.864.9289 • Open Mon–Sat 11 a.m.–10 p.m.

Stella's Hamburgers 106 Galvin Road South • Bellevue, NE
402.291.6088 • Open Mon–Fri 11 a.m.–8 p.m. • Sat 11 a.m.–3 p.m.

Taylor's Maid-Rite 106 South Third Avenue • Marshalltown, IA
641.753.9684 • Open Mon–Sat 8 a.m.–10 p.m. • Sun 10 a.m.–10 p.m.

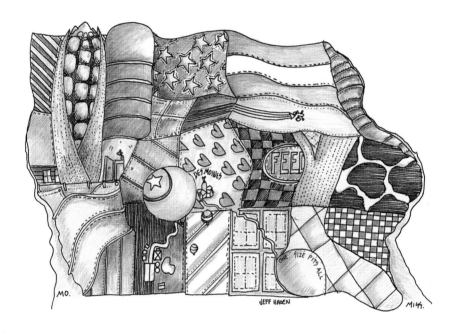

About the Author
Jeff Hagen

Jeff Hagen is a best-selling author of six published books, including two award winners: Steeple Chase, which he also illustrated, and Hiawatha Passing. The latter was acclaimed by numerous critics, including the Milwaukee Journal, Publishers Weekly, Kirkus Reviews, N.E.A., the Junior Library Guild of America, and the New York Times, which honored it as one of the ten best children's books in America (1995).

Jeff also writes and illustrates cover stories and travel features for many regional and national newspapers, including the Chicago Tribune, St. Paul Pioneer Press, Sunday Detroit News, Minneapolis Star Tribune, Wisconsin State Journal, Capital Times, and Milwaukee Journal Sentinel. His stories and artwork have appeared in Wisconsin Trails, Cricket, and Outside magazines. Internationally, his work has appeared in the Beijing Review in the People's Republic of China.

He is in frequent demand as a guest speaker and storyteller at public schools, libraries and universities. His paintings and drawings have appeared in juried shows and exhibits across the United States and Europe. His artwork is part of the permanent collection of the American Embassy in Oslo, Norway.

He also makes appearances as guest author on the Wisconsin Public Radio Network and his books have been featured on TV's Food Channel and Good Morning America.

Who knows? Maybe I'll see you in the next booth.

Alas, shortly into my journey and quest, I realized that I just couldn't get them all. So, here's an invitation to you: if I missed your favorite grill, state the issue in a letter and send it to Jeff Hagen, c/o Adventure Publications, 820 Cleveland St. S., Cambridge, MN 55008. I will try to head out to your place on the map, sit down and indulge in "that one-of-a-kind hamburger" at "that one-of-a-kind place."